Jakub

Jakub

The boy with a dream to fly

Jakub Bilicki

ISBN: 9798375303789

Firstly, I would like to dedicate this book to my family & friends.

Secondly, to my secondary school teacher Mrs. Leese who was a big inspiration in writing this book.

All the best!

Jakub

Dear Reader

Welcome!

Firstly, I would like to thank you for buying my book. Or if you were gifted this book then a big 'thank you' to whoever gifted you this.

Why did I write this book?

By writing this book I aim to let people explore my past with me. I will also talk about how my passion for my hobby got so strong that nothing will be able to stop me from loving it. Lastly, I will talk about my hopes for the future and a very important person that has impacted all of this.

Contents

1.
Taking a step back

I must admit aviation was not my only strong hobby throughout my life. When I was about 7 or 8, I always remember being extremely interested in public transportation. The city where I grew up has over 100 years of history in its public transport sector, but out of everything that the city used as part of its public transport scheme it was the trams that would roam the city that would always catch my attention. Buses also meant a lot to me but not as much as the trams did.

Whenever I stepped in a tram it was like entering a whole new world. The feeling of it shake as it was going through some uneven tracks or the warm air blasting on you as soon as you entered one of the old red trams in the summer and the chilling air during winter, which for some passengers made the journey a dreadful one. However, having an unpleasant journey was not the case for me. The next stop announcements were the only thing keeping me in the real world.

My passion grew even stronger when a new tram line opened on the opposite side of my parents' restaurant. It sometimes felt like paradise on earth watching the buses and trams go past every day. Of course, I was not that obsessed with public communication to the point where I would not talk or do anything else. Though, I did feel that it was a part of me. I would sometimes sit in front of the restaurant and watch each bus and tram stop and go as the passengers either got on or off. It felt special to me being able to have a front row experience of my hobby.

On a cold winter evening in December with snow falling down a group of tram drivers stopped at the tram stop with their trams during some tests and came to our restaurant for some food. I happened to be at the restaurant that day and they noticed me looking at the trams through the window. This led to them asking me if I would want to go with them to have a look at the tram whilst the food was being prepared. Of course, my answer was ‘Yes!’.

Together we went towards the tram stop to let me explore one of them. It was a new type that not a single passenger was able to be on yet. I was the very first person to step foot in one and it felt amazing! The tram itself was so much more modern compared to the ones that would roam the city. It had TV screens that would tell you where exactly you are and all the information you would need about your journey. At the end I was invited for a picture in the tram driver cabin, I even got to ring the bell at the tram in front of us. It was a very special moment that would be treasured forever.

One day I decided to risk a lot. I was so interested with the whole public communication system that I decided that I should get from my school to the restaurant all by myself. After waiting to be picked up outside of school for about 10 minutes I started to make a move. I also had no way of contacting my parents as I left my phone at home that day.

I walked to the crossing where our school lollipop lady would help us cross the road. She asked me what happened that I was walking by myself, and I replied by saying that this was a one off situation. She laughed and I carried on with my journey. On my way home one of my neighbours drove past and stopped to offer me a lift to our house. I accepted as I knew the lady very well. She dropped me off and I walked up to the door. My auntie was at home babysitting my brother but then I realised that I should surprise my parents by making my way to their restaurant.

Without thinking about it twice I made my way to the bus stop and waited for the correct bus to arrive. Soon the bus arrived, and I got on. By now I was thinking of not getting caught for not having a ticket for the ride. About 15 minutes later I was getting off the bus just like the people that I would watch and made my way inside the restaurant. Surprisingly my parents were not there so I knew something was up. It was made even more obvious when the waitress called my parents that I was with her.

Walking back and forwards I was waiting for my parents to get back. As the restaurant car park was at the back of it, I would walk up to the door and every few minutes look if they were finally there. Until one time I opened the door and saw that instead of my parents' car there was a police car parked up. I realised that they were in fact looking for me whilst I was enjoying myself with my hobby. Shortly after my parents arrived, and I was not in the good books for a little while.

At this time, I did not really have any close contact with planes except for the ones that I would see in the sky every now and again. I have never travelled abroad at this point and have only seen a plane land at the airport once or twice, but every time I did see one it was something surreal. I still remember when LOT Polish Airlines were training their pilots on the new Boeing 787 Dreamliner, and it went right over my head seconds before making contact with the airport runway.

However, then came the year 2016 and unfortunately the restaurant had to be closed. I would be lying if I said that the restaurant was not at least a small part of me. It always was and always will be, so when it closed it was like losing a piece of myself. It also meant that I lost that everyday sight of my hobby which I loved so much.

2.
A new beginning

A few months have flown by since the closure of the restaurant. We did not know what was going to happen next, will my parents go back to a 9 to 5 job? Or will the restaurant soon be reopened? However, it soon became clear that none of these options would come true and little did I know that in those few month's plans were being made to move to a new home in a completely different country, England.

Soon came November of 2016, I do not remember the exact day, but November was the month that my dad moved to the UK. He was the first from my family to start a new life somewhere else. I missed him lots during this time and his absence could be felt everywhere. Although I did have a small hope inside me that he would soon come back to Poland, and we could continue our life as normal. Unfortunately, as I later found out this would not be the case...

Around a week before Christmas, I found out that it was now my time to move to the UK, I could not believe it. It was a mixture of emotions. I felt saddened but also excited that I will be able to experience life in a new country. Shortly, I told my friends the big news and they too could not believe it. I had a great friend group, but I was sure that nobody would ever be able to replace them (this does not mean I would not meet some great people along the way here in England). Yet another piece of myself was lost.

I felt like my world was slowly falling apart, piece by piece.

It was scary having to think about the idea of not being able to see my grandparents every weekend or not being able to go and meet up with my friends who were like family to me, but most of all having to think about the idea of leaving my country Poland. It was terrifying.

Very shortly came the 26th of December 2016, moving day to the UK and a new beginning in my life but not so much my passion yet. It was an early day with lots of crying from the moment I woke up. I remember that day like it was yesterday. Being at the airport waiting in an awfully long security line for an airport with only 3 or 4 destinations at the time. Sometimes with just one departure per day.

The airport was also the first time I was aware of an encounter with a British person, and it was a funny one. At least for me... maybe not so much if I was the woman shouting.

"Let me get past please! My flight is leaving soon".

And somehow making her way to the very front of the security line. To this day I still hope that she made it for her flight to London, but I will never know.

After a bit of a wait, we were finally past security and waiting for our flight. The flight was from Bydgoszcz to Birmingham, but at the time I had no clue which part of the UK I was going to, this also meant that I did not really know what to expect when I arrived. When boarding the plane, the last person to say goodbye to us was the boarding agent who turned out to be my mom's friend.

Strangely, I do not remember lots from the flight, maybe due to the roller coaster of emotions I was going through, happiness, sadness, and excitement all at the same time. One of the only parts I do remember from this flight is the take-off and the moment I was glued to the seat from the rapid acceleration of the plane. Very faintly I also remember the landing but not so much that I can recall what happened.

The flight lasted for about 2 hours (I only know this because I still fly on the same route quite often whenever visiting my family in Poland). Once again something that I remember like it was yesterday, a lengthy line again but this time for border control. When stepping outside the terminal the first thing I was met with was the 'amazing' British weather. Not the most welcoming as you can imagine.

We were picked up by my parents' friend and got driven from Birmingham to Stoke where we arrived at our new house. I was extremely excited for this part as I have never lived in anything other than a flat (since they are common in big cities in Poland and most of Europe), so it was a new experience for me.

3.
Welcome to England!

It must have been late in the evening by the time I arrived in Stoke on Trent, or it could have just been a dark and rainy winter afternoon.

I still remember walking into the house for the first time and seeing all the things from Poland waiting in boxes to be opened. It felt as if not only we moved but our house moved with us. However, I must say that it was nice to see those things as they always made me feel a little bit more at home.

Most importantly we were back together again...

After eating and familiarizing ourselves with our new house we decided to head out with the hope of doing some grocery shopping at Tesco. We put our coats on and set off on our way. Little did we know that this walk would turn into a mission of finding Tesco. It must have been at least a 40-minute walk (we did not have a car at the time) to get to Hanley but finding Tesco was the difficult part. We must have spent about 10 minutes looking for it with no success, so we decided to head back home and stop in a corner shop with Polish food in that we saw on our way to Hanley.

The next day we decided to have a go at finding Tesco again. Luckily, this time we were successful, and it turned out that we were only about 2 minutes away from it the day before.

4.
Back to School

As we moved to England during the Christmas school holidays, we had to wait until January to get me signed up for school. It was only a few days after New Year's Eve when I went with my parents to get me signed up for primary school.

Everyone was very welcoming from the very first second in the building but anxiously I was waiting for a meeting with the principal. Luckily there was a Polish teacher that worked at the school which made communication easier for me.

To this day I still remember one question that I was asked,

"What do you like outside of school?"

I did not have to think for long about my answer and started to list all the possible methods of public transportation with trams being my number one on my list, at the time planes did not make it onto the list. Most likely because I only flew on one about a week ago and did not know how big my passion for them would grow in the coming years. I also still remember the extreme look of terror and confusion on the principal's face when she found out that I am extremely passionate about public transport, something you would not expect from an 8 year old child. Or as I later figured out, she might not have had the same experience of public communication as me. Afterall, the public transport in Stoke was nothing compared to the one in Poland.

I was then given a tour of the school which turned out to be not what I expected. Firstly, all the classrooms were separated into year groups meaning no class movement. Secondly, one teacher handled every subject you learned. Thirdly, lessons were an hour, not 45 minutes as I was used to, and a school day always started and finished at the same time. One last thing I was surprised about was the school uniform which I have never yet experienced and made me feel quite restricted.

However, I was accepted and told to come back next Monday. One thing I was confused about was that I was put in year 4 and not year 3 like I was in Poland, but from what I know it is the same in both countries. I do have to admit that I felt quite cool with that and always went around saying.

“I missed a year of education!”

because of the class move. Maybe not so good if I think about it.

5.
New school, new experience

It was a cold and dark Monday morning in January, not the way you want to start your first day at a new school. However, I was overly excited for this day!

I put on my uniform, and I must admit that I felt like a small businessman. Though I would not say that the uniform was suitable for business, at least not the businessman I always envisioned.

The school day started at 8:45am and I needed to leave the house by 7:45am. Unluckily, we lived about an hour walk away from my school, which was not ideal. At the time we still did not have a car but even if we did, we would have to walk anyway. This is because my dad started work at 6am and my mom could not drive (and still does not drive to this day), I wonder when she will drive if ever... However, this did mean having to wake up at stupid o'clock just to get ready and make my way to school.

It was time to leave the house and without a surprise, it was raining outside. Typical British weather at its finest but we had no choice other than to walk. We walked for what felt like forever. I thought that we would never ever get to my school. Although we eventually got there, it was a considerable success, I think.

I walked through the school doors and made my way to the classroom. I put my things onto the coat hanger, sat down at my table and was ready to see what would come next.

There was yet another surprise on the very first day, there were no bells in between lessons. I must really say that schools are quite different in Poland and England. And then yet another surprise, an assembly, something I have never heard of before or experienced. My first day at a new school was a unique experience but also a memorable one.

Throughout my first week at school more surprises kept on coming my way. Longer lunch breaks, instead of 20 minutes we got a whole hour. Three assemblies per week, with the Friday one being a rewards assembly. It was great to see everyone's success being celebrated so often.

I felt very welcome by the end of the week and was already enjoying school here more than in Poland. I still would never go back to education in Poland to this day.

6.
Wales

The 25th of February is my mom's birthday. We have been in England for almost two months, and we just did what everyday people would. However, we felt that it was time to get out and do something.

As our first trip ever, we went to Conwy Castle in Wales. At the time I was very confused about the idea of only being a two hour drive away from a new country which also has the same currency as England. I really did not make those connections with the same currency being used in multiple countries, something that I am not confused about now.

It was an amazing day out but how could it have been a day without a new surprise. When walking around the castle I happened to look out of a window in one of the towers and to my surprise the riverbed was dry. At this point I asked myself,

"How is it possible that the river is dry in February?"

I even asked my parents, but they too were not sure why that was happening.

It must have been about 10-15 minutes later when I looked out one of the windows again and saw that the river was there as if nothing ever happened. I was in a state of confusion with the 'phenomenon' that occurred, but I made it my mission to find out what happened. To my surprise England has tides due to its connection with the ocean and that the dry riverbed was a low tide and when the water appeared it was a high tide. Fascinating!

After we finished the tour of the castle it was time to explore the small town. I remember coming across my first red telephone booth and of course I had to get photos with it. Although the smell inside it was not so pleasant, I was happy with the photos that I got.

My first visit to Wales was an amazing one and I was sure to come back again!

7.

More and more trips (2017)

Ever since we went to Wales in February, we had more and more trips coming our way.

In April of 2017 we went to Llandudno. Here we got the experience of the Great Orme Tramway. It was a unique experience being pulled up the Great Orme summit by cable trams and the only ones in operation in Britain.

In June of 2017 we visited Southport. This is where if I said to someone that the sea disappeared people would believe it. It took us at least two hours to reach the sea and I would not be surprised if the distance to get there was over 1km. However, as we later found out the tides are so strong here that they go more than a kilometre out at low tide and when it is high tide they come to the very shore.

In early August of 2017 we visited Bristol. Here we went onboard SS Great Britain. I felt like I was sailing back in the 19th century. Whenever you walked into one of the facilities onboard the ship you felt like everything around you was really happening. When you walked into the bakery you would smell the fresh bread being baked or when you walked into 3rd class you could barely breathe.

We also went onto the Clifton Suspension Bridge as part of our visit to Bristol. I must say that walking over 100 meters above the river Avon was not the best experience I had. You should have seen my face when I found out we must go back across it to get to our car. Luckily for me I 'survived' and enjoyed the experience. It was not that bad if I was enjoying it.

In late August of 2017 we went for our summer holidays in Poland! It was great finally feeling a bit more at home. However, I will never forget the experience of having to go all the way to Poland by car. Especially when the car was a small Citroen C3, and the journey was about 24 hours. This was my worst car journey ever.

In September of 2017 we visited the monkeys at Knowsley Safari Park. I remember sitting in the car and driving through the safari. Even though one of the naughty monkeys 'injured' our car it was still an amazing experience.

And that was it for the trips of 2017, it was a year filled with lots of adventures.

8.
Holy Communion

May of 2018 was the time of my Holy Communion. You would think that because I lived in England, I would have to do it in English. However, luckily for me there is a Polish church in Stoke which made me able to have it in Polish.

I think everyone in my family would agree that May was a busy month. Firstly, came my auntie and cousin. Unfortunately, they could not stay for the communion, but it was still great to have them here. I remember when they arrived at Manchester Airport and the terminal they arrived at had a bomb threat, not an experience I would want to go through.

About a week later (a few days before my communion) my auntie and cousin left. They were 'replaced' with my grandma's and grandad's. It was great to have them all here!

9.
Grandma's Wild Stay

In July of 2018, my grandma came to England for her 'wild stay'. It was about mid-July when we booked a one-way ticket for her to England, sounds fun right? Well, since she did not have a ticket back to Poland, she was here in England for over a month. However, I would say that we had some good adventures during this month.

Firstly, we once again visited Llandudno and took the Great Orme Tramway. Even though we have been there before it was great to go there once again.

Secondly, we visited Liverpool and got a photo with The Beatles (statues of course) and walked around the waterfront. Truly magnificent but even better in the evening when everything was lit up.

Two weeks later we went to visit the Queen's residence at Windsor Castle. The queue for tickets must have been at least 2 hours. Though, it was great to see lots of places around the castle.

After those three trips we spent the rest of our time at home and after about a month and a half grandma went back to Poland.

10.
New Passion Unlocked

Let us fast track to February of 2019. During the February half-term, we went to Poland. This was to get new passports but also to visit our family.

This was the point where I felt like a new passion in aviation was unlocked. I think this happened because I no longer had that contact with the public transport in Poland that I liked so much so I thought it was time to move on. It just happened to be aviation that stood out so much to me.

Ever since those two flights I have become so passionate about aviation that I think nothing else will be able to ever replace it. However, this is not me saying I just lost all my passion in public transportation. Of course not. Whenever I go to Poland, I take photos of the trams and buses just like I would of airplanes at the airport.

This was also the time that I got my first plane model ever. An Emirates A380. Which soon triggered me to keep on expanding my collection.

11.
Goodbye Primary School

In July of 2019 my primary school life was coming to an end. Throughout my three years of attending, I was able to create lots of memories and I was able to meet lots of amazing people.

Even though at the very start of my learning I was at a disadvantage because of the language barrier I was able to make my way to the very top.

However, at the end of year 6 I was incredibly lucky to receive the top marks for my SATs results. Quite clearly, I must have been a good learner.

I also still remember when I found out which secondary school I will be going to a few months before leaving primary school. When I found out I cried for the rest of the evening. These tears were not happy tears, they were tears of sadness and anger. My reaction for my secondary school wasn't the best because I got given my 3rd choice, not something that you want. Afterall it was the school I wanted to go to the least.

12.
Exploring Poland

In August 2019 it was time for our holiday in Poland and it was going to be a fun one.

As always, for our summer holiday we travelled by car. Luckily at this point we had a new and bigger Ford Titanium, meaning our journey comfort was also significantly improved. We travelled through multiple counties including France, Belgium, The Netherlands and Germany before finally reaching Poland.

Normally on our long drive we would have an overnight stop in Germany. However, this time we decided to be brave and not have one. The experience of driving without a stop overnight did teach us a lesson, always stay the night in Germany.

Eventually it took us about a day and a half to reach Poland. We were exhausted.

I was very excited to finally get to my grandparents' house because I was planning on buying my second ever plane model. This time I decided that it should be a Ryanair model. Afterall it was the first airline that I ever flew with. It was ordered but my face dropped when I found out that I would have to visit two other cities before I got it. This was because the next day after our arrival we were leaving for Cracow (Kraków).

Up first on our list of places to visit was Cracow (Kraków). We've never been to the city before, so it sounded like an amazing plan. After our over 24 hour drive the day before another 7 hour drive was coming up.

Personally, the drive to Cracow (Kraków) felt much worse than the drive to Poland. Possibly because the motorway was shut so we had to take the slow village roads. We arrived late in the evening, so we decided to stay in the hotel and get some rest.

During our time in Cracow (Kraków) we had lots of fun. We explored the old town which was fabulous.

A key part of our visit to Cracow (Kraków) was the Wawel Castle. This was the monarch's residence whilst they ruled in Poland. It is argued to be the most culturally and historically significant site in Poland. The castle was amazing to walk around, and it was built in lots of different architectural styles from all around Europe.

Secondly, we visited the Wieliczka Salt Mine which is now classed as a UNESCO World Heritage Site. I must say I did put a finger on the wall and then lick it to see if it was salty and it sure was. The mine was huge and just to get about halfway down must have taken at least 30 minutes. We had to take the stairs down, but this just added to the experience.

Whilst we were down exploring the mine, we got to see some beautiful things. One of the main things that really impressed me must have been the St Kinga's Chapel inside the mine and it wasn't a small one. Possibly, the size of a small church. I was also quite surprised to see a bright blue lake inside.

To my surprise the total length of the salt mine is over 280 km (178 miles). The visitor route covers less than 2% of the whole mine at about 3.5km (2.2 miles)

We then spent the next few days relaxing in Cracow (Kraków) before heading up north to the sea.

It was soon time to head up north to the seaside of Poland. We had a long journey ahead of us again, practically going across the whole of Poland.

On our way we were determined to stop at 'Czestochowa Jasna Góra' which is the holiest place in Poland. Located here is the picture of Our Lady of Czestochowa which attracts millions of pilgrims and tourists every year.

However, the very warm weather did not help. Not only were we exhausted from spending the day in our car and the hot temperatures, but our car also gave in. Unlucky for us. About two hours away from our destination our car started to often overheat. This meant that we had to take stops along the motorway for it to cool down. We kept doing this until it got so bad that we couldn't drive it anymore.

We tried to get towed, but we couldn't until the next day. There was no way that this would ruin our holiday. Of course not. So, my grandad came to the rescue. He drove all the way out to us onto the motorway so that he could take us to his house.

Before the car broke down, we were hoping to arrive at my grandparents' house by 9pm but in the end we arrived at around 1am. What a lovely day!

A few days later it was time to head out for some attractions.

During our time at the seaside, we mainly visited the Słowiński National Park. Here we got to climb some tall sand dunes with some reaching about 30m above sea level. As I stood on the sand dune, I had a different view wherever I looked. To my left I had an amazing view onto the Baltic Sea and to my right I had a view onto a forest. Even though the climb was tiring I thought it was a fabulous experience.

Throughout the next few days of our seaside stay we visited the beach quite a few times.

Soon came the next adventure. I must admit it was a naughty one. We went urban exploring in a no trespassing area. Our exploration took place at Łapalice Castle. This was a castle which construction was never finished, most likely due to running out of money. Now when you think of a castle then you think of the monarchy. This was not the case here. The castle was all privately funded but never finished. It was most likely meant to serve as a home just on a much larger scale.

Interestingly, the castle was built in such a way it would have a strong connection to the calendar. It would have as many towers as months in the year. Then it would have as many halls as weeks in a year and lastly as many windows as days in a year.

Even though the construction was never completed it was still an amazing experience.

Once our car got fixed, we headed back to Bydgoszcz where we spent a few days. Afterwards, we set off on our way back to England.

13.
First time properly plane spotting

Without even realising my passion for aviation grew stronger and stronger. In late August of 2019 I downloaded the 'all-time favourite app among plane spotters' Flightradar 24. This new app 'discovery' led me to always be looking at the very frequent departures and arrivals at Manchester Airport.

One morning I looked up at the clear summer sky and realised just how many planes fly over me in a very short time. I was fascinated about just how close my hobby was to me.

My passion only kept getting stronger and stronger. Nothing would be able to break the bond now.

Coincidentally or not during this short period of time I came across a YouTube channel which was posting plane spotting videos from Manchester Airport. This gave me inspiration to go there myself and take photos of the rapid plane movements.

After a few days of discussing this idea with my parents I was finally given the big YES and we all agreed that I could go to the airport to get some amazing photos. Amazing at the time at least, now I take more 'professional' photos with my camera.

I decided that the best idea to prepare for my first-time plane spotting would be to write down all the arriving and departing planes in my notebook. Afterall, I did not know what my first experience would be like. I promised myself to write this a day in advance as the Flight radar 24 schedules only get released about 24 hours in advance. As it turned out I completely forgot to do this.

However, the important day finally came.

Even though for many people this would look like a small thing, for me it was something big. As I forgot to do the arrival and departure list I thought it would be a good idea to quickly write it on the morning. I thought I would make a huge use of it once at the airport but as it later turned out I didn't even look at it once. I never did this again after!

At around 10am we finally set off to Manchester Airport. After about an hour drive, we were finally at the car park close to my chosen place for plane spotting. Although we had another 15 minutes to walk before we were there.

As we were walking, I could hear but not see the planes taking off from the runway on the other side of the hill. I had a feeling that this would be the perfect spot close to the planes.

14.
New School, Levelling Up

With my primary school life finishing back in July 2019 it was now time to level up. I still could not believe I am going to my 3rd choice school. I felt like I was going through my worst nightmare. Little did I know that soon I would regret everything I ever said about the school.

In September of 2019 a new journey began in secondary school.

On my first day I took the earliest bus I have ever taken; it came at around 7:20am and school started at 9am. I was very determined not to be late on my first day. Though, I must have gotten to school about an hour early. I promised myself to get the later bus from the next day...

Although, I had mixed feelings about my first day at school, I was very excited to see what would come at me.

First things first I walked into the wrong part of the school and sat in the cafeteria not in the auditorium where we were meant to be having an assembly. Not the start I was expecting, and this did panic me a little bit but luckily the panic was soon over when I found the right place. Very quickly I figured out why I didn't go there in the first place. I arrived at school so early that the doors to the auditorium were still closed so nobody told me that I should be in there.

After the 'Welcome Assembly' it was time to go and spend some time in form. Most of the morning was spent with my amazing form tutor talking about the expectations around school and writing some prayers as it was a Catholic school.

Soon came break time and then time for my first lesson. It was my least favourite subject, mathematics. I must admit that my teacher during the 'bootcamp' sessions was a funny person. She even had math equations on her shoes. Unfortunately, they didn't help with assessments. I had two more lessons that day but can't remember what they were.

Overall, I felt very happy after the first day!

15.
Memorable flight

As per our tradition of going to Poland in February it was time to visit again. This time I remember the specific departure date. It was the 18th of February 2020, and the flight meant a lot to me. It was also the time when I felt that my passion just carried on getting stronger.

A few weeks prior to the flight I saw Ryanair post a story of a man who flew with them and gave a letter to the pilots asking for details of the flight. This really inspired me and I thought that I could do the same. Soon I had written my letter, printed it and it was ready to fly with me. I was really excited to see if I would get a reply or not.

This time my dad was not travelling with us, but we were hoping to all go together to Poland during summer. At the time we had no idea how serious COVID-19 would get.

As we were entering the security check area my mum noticed someone that she recognised from a Polish TV series that she always watches. He seemed to be having some problems with the lady at security with a squishy hammer toy that he was carrying. To be clear I've had previous experience with that lady at the airport and she was never nice, so I felt bad for him. However, I couldn't do anything so just carried on with my business.

We went through security with no problems, and we were finally airside (this is the area after security checks and where the gates are located). There were quite a few empty seats as it was an evening flight, so we found ourselves a seat and waited for our gate to be announced. Personally, I felt like the gate was announced very late.

However, as we were waiting the actor once again appeared. He was sat down about three rows away from us. I confirmed with my mum that it was him and not somebody that looked very similar. As we were unsure of his name, we thought that we would double check the cast and find him. Shortly we found him, and it was the one and only Wojtek Rotowski.

With a bit of hesitation and stress I decided to approach him. I walked up to him and asked for an autograph and a picture. At the end I got both, very successful. He was really cool and all the stress that I had disappeared by the time I was finished speaking with him. Whilst we were waiting, I was wondering if he was on the same flight as us.

About 30 minutes later our boarding gate was finally announced. We got up and made our way there with a quick stop at the toilet before the flight. It was now time to focus on my mission with the letter for the pilots. I was getting more and more excited.

Luckily, we were one of the first people to board the aircraft. Whilst on the apron I quickly decided that I wouldn't give the letter to the flight attendant myself and ask them to pass it on. I was stressed out. Instead after some quick persuading my mum did it for me.

The flight attendant was lovely and said that she will pass the letter on. A strange thought passed through my head that she never actually gave it because she forgot during boarding. This thought was also triggered because I never saw her go to the front of the aircraft. I could have missed her going to the front or she gave it at a different point.

About half-way through the flight the same flight attendant came to me. She said that the captain is inviting me to the cockpit at the end of the flight. At this point the flight became the best one I ever had. I couldn't wait to visit the cockpit at the end.

After landing and arriving at our gate we waited for everyone to disembark so that we would be the last people off the plane. I went to the cockpit to get my letter and get a picture of it. To my surprise it was smaller than I could have ever imagined.

The picture I took could have been lots better, but the pilot waved his hand as he was showing something to the first officer and I unfortunately managed to take that one and only photo. I didn't even realise until we left the airport. I felt happy but also a little bit annoyed.

16.
Last time in Poland for a while

After my amazing and memorable flight, it was time to enjoy the one week stay in Poland and make the most out of it. As per usual we stayed in two cities as my family lives in the surrounding cities of Gdańsk and in Bydgoszcz where I come from.

Unfortunately, this time we didn't have many things planned to do but rather just rest and enjoy our time. However, this doesn't mean we didn't have any fun things to do.

Coincidentally, whilst we were in Gdańsk with my grandparents and my auntie it was Fat Thursday. Meaning we had to eat lots of doughnuts. I must admit that they were the best doughnuts I ever ate. Of course, locally found by my grandad.

The day that we were flying out on was my mum's birthday and it was mandatory to go for a birthday dinner during our stay. The chosen restaurant was a Georgian one which we were introduced to during summer of 2019. I felt like I was eating the best food ever. Something that looks like pizza but isn't with four different Georgian cheeses on it. Or dough sacks filled with meat and soup. Yum! The best part was of course the dessert. A hot brownie with vanilla ice cream...

Overall, we did not spend lots of time out on activities. We mostly enjoyed some quality time with our family.

On the 25th of February it was unfortunately time to fly back to England. I was going to give my spare letter that I had from the week to the pilot. However, it had all the wrong details on. It said that I was flying out to Poland when I was actually flying back to England! I just couldn't give it. I felt a bit angry about it but there was nothing that I could do.

Strangely, I didn't take single picture during that flight, only a video of the landing. I would probably say this was because my passion was starting to go into full gear at this moment. Even more than after my flight in February of 2019.

After coming back to England all of us had no idea just how much the world would change in the coming months and how much our lives would be touched by what was to come.

17.
COVID

Towards the end of March about a month after coming back from Poland the unexpected happened. England the same as most of the world was put under a national lockdown due to the quickly spreading pandemic. Nobody knew what will happen in the coming days, weeks and even months. All we knew was that it wouldn't get better for a while.

Within a short period of the lockdown announcement online school started. I had mixed feelings about it. I felt like I would be able to lay out my day the way I really wanted to, which did not happen. However, I also felt like I would get less learning done due to the amount of 'better things to do' I would find for myself, which was the option I went with.

I won't hide it that during these lessons I would often switch them on and then do something else. The lessons would sometimes become a background noise. Although, some teachers did find a way to stop people (including me) from not engaging in their lessons. One teacher wouldn't believe you were in the lesson unless you answered at least one question. I think this was a smart but sometimes annoying idea. Luckily, only one or two teachers did it and they were the subjects I liked most.

I carried on with online learning as I had no choice. It was the new version of school.

Towards the end of Year 7 which was fully online it was time to go back to school but not to learn. It was time when I would see my form tutor and see the 'progress' I made during the year. If there was any. To my surprise I did make some progress which I was pleased with.

As it was the beginning of the summer holidays, I started to get very annoyed with the fact that I would have to spend even some of it inside. Even though I knew we were going on holiday to Cornwall.

However, the few weeks approaching our holiday went past somewhat quickly and we were finally packing for our holiday. I was buzzing with excitement.

18.
Summer in Cornwall

In early August it was finally time to pack for our holiday in Cornwall. Even though we were not going to a different country I felt like I was going to have a great time even on holiday in the UK.

We left in the early morning hours to get to Cornwall for the evening. Afterall, we had a 6 hour drive to get there. We were almost going to the most southern point in the UK often referred to as Land's End. We were only 30 minutes away from it.

The town that we chose to stay in was called Hayle. To make the holiday even more fun we decided that we would take our family friends along with us. The holiday house that we stayed in had the best view I have ever seen. The windows spread across the whole wall revealing a beautiful view of St. Ives Bay, we could even see St. Ives itself on the other side of the bay. It was beautiful.

Throughout the week we explored Cornwall.

There were countless beaches that we visited. I must say that the one that was directly connected with the Atlantic Ocean was the one with the most violent waves.

The scenery across the whole of Cornwall was beautiful.

On our last day the weather across Cornwall was very foggy and gloomy. Not something you would expect on your holiday in August. However, it was still in England, so anything was possible. On that morning I opened the curtain to reveal the amazing view as I did each morning, but it wasn't there. It was such a disappointment as the fog covered everything up.
This wouldn't stop us from our plans though. We stopped off at Land's End hoping that we would get an amazing view onto the Atlantic Ocean. Although this did not happen as it was still very foggy. I can't complain though as we did get a chance to take a picture with the famous sign there.

What I found interesting during the holiday in Cornwall was just how many planes flew over us going to many different places around the world. Even though I wasn't on one of those flights I was happy to see them fly over me as it is my passion.

After an exciting week in Cornwall, it was unfortunately time to return home. It looked like I would be once again stuck at home doing nothing.

19.
How long will normality last?

Soon after our holiday in August it was announced that we would be going back to school. I felt happy but also disappointed that I would no longer lay out my day the way I wanted to.

Our hopes of returning to normality were getting higher. However, nobody was sure how long this would last.

In the first week of September, I went back to school. It felt good to be finally standing in its walls. Maybe I would be able to catch up on what I missed in Year 7. Or at least to some extent. School did change quite a bit. Each year group was now in a different part of the school. Teachers would come to us instead of us coming to them. Lunchtimes were different for each year group too. Something that didn't change though were the people that I was surrounded with.

For the next few months, we carried on coming to school every day as normal. I was finally back in the rhythm of doing so. Until one day we were back to online learning. Again! Just as I got used to being in school. At this point I was fuming.

We now had an answer to our question too. Normality did not last long.

Online learning carried on all the way up until the Christmas school break. Although before Christmas came, I had a very important step forward in my hobby.

20.
Proper plane spotter

During the October school break I thought it would be a good idea to head to the airport for some plane spotting. Afterall, I haven't been for over a year. We still went to Manchester Airport but this time to the Runway Visitor Park where the famous Concorde is located.

Firstly, I went and did my plane spotting with my dad's phone. I felt like he had the best quality pictures and much more storage that I had. I saw some big planes even closer than I did previously. I had a fun day out.

The next day, I started to look for a camera so that I could take more professional and amazing photos. I found a reasonably priced camera that came with two lenses already! I was amazed. Although, I could not get it myself, I had to ask my parents. My dad agreed with it straight away. After some persuading my mum agreed too. Life was going perfectly.

A few days later my camera arrived. As I could not go to the airport straight away, I decided that the best thing to do would be some plane spotting but from my bedroom window. From this moment I would always be looking out at the sky for some planes flying over. Luckily for me planes that would be either approaching or departing Manchester Airport and East Midlands Airport would always fly overhead. What more could I want?

Of course, I couldn't just sit and take photos of planes at high altitudes all the time. I had to try out my new camera at the airport. So off we went.

It felt so much nicer knowing that the photos I took would be of much higher quality. Now even though back then I thought that the photos I took where the best I would not say the same 3 years later. I feel like my photos are much better. And, to many people this would not be much, it's just a photo after all but I felt like I was getting closer and closer to my passion.

21.
Thank you for the memories!

I remember this day just like it was yesterday. On the 31 December 2020 we were meant to be celebrating the arrival of 2021. Hopefully a much better year. However, very soon it would become the complete opposite.

Just before 10am a new plane model that I ordered arrived. I was excited as I was saving up to buy it for a while. It was a Qatar 787 Dreamliner. I did get disappointed with it as one tiny part came off from it, but I decided not to make a fuss and let it stay in my collection.

About an hour after I opened my new fantastic plane model my mom got a terrifying phone call from Poland.

A few days before New Year's Eve my grandparents tested positive for COVID-19. I was really hoping that they would get well very soon, and things would only get better and not worse. This however was not the case. My grandad become so ill that he had to be taken to hospital. I could not believe what was happening. Something that we only ever saw on TV was now happening within our family.

Progressively, my grandad's condition was getting worse and worse. Until one day it got better, to the point where he called my grandma to say that he is feeling better. However, this did not last for long. The next day he was feeling bad once again. My whole family was hoping that he would feel better and return home.

After a week of intensive care and fighting for life my grandad, who I strongly looked up to, unfortunately passed away. It was a huge loss for everyone. Would life ever get back to normal now…

On the very same day that we learnt that my grandad passed away we had to find a way to get to Poland for the funeral. We figured that the best way would be to take the car. As by now we had an SUV we knew that the ride will be more comfortable. Although I would get back into the very first car we had, just to be there for my grandad.
All of this happened when restrictions were still in place and for us to cross the French border we had to get a COVID test. I will never forget when I had to get the stick 'shoved' up my nose. It made my eyes tear up.

The next day we set off on our way to Poland. The roads in every country were very empty. Partially because each country had restrictions in place but also because there was quite a bit of snow about. In just under 24 hours, we were at my aunties house in Poland.

We arrived on my little brother's birthday so of course we had some delicious cake lined up. Yum! However, the loss of my grandad could be felt in the air.

One day in the middle of winter we decided that we should go to the beach. Yes, you read that right, to the beach. Even though we would not do anything there I still found it cool. It showed me a different perspective to the beach that would normally be full of people and warm of course. To my surprise there were even people in the sea. I could feel how cold they would be without even touching the sea.

Very quickly came 15 January 2021, the day of the funeral. It was snowing a whole lot outside. I had snow above my ankles at some points. I could not remember the last time I saw some much of it. Nevertheless, that was not the important part of the day, my grandad was more important.

My whole family walked into the church and made our way to the front rows. Naturally we were all sat there in tears. A pack of tissues each was almost not enough. There was a photo of my grandad stood at the front of the church and whenever I looked at it I thought it was smiling at me. Of course, that was my imagination playing up.

At the end of the mass my family were the first people to walk out. Throughout the mass I did not turn around even once. As we were leaving, I was stunned to see how many people turned up. It was a full Church. Even the neighbours somehow found out about our loss and turned up. Overall, I felt like my grandad had a proper last goodbye.

22.
Cornwall 2021

As there were still restrictions in other countries across Europe, we decided that we would go back to Cornwall for summer again instead of going to Poland. However, I won't hide it that Poland was a plan B right until the day that we went to Cornwall. You never know when the restrictions would change. This time we went by ourselves without our family friends.

When we were in Cornwall the year before we missed out on some great sightseeing opportunities, due to not pre-booking tickets, which we really regretted. This time we promised ourselves that we would visit as many of the things that we missed as possible.

Up first on our list was Minack Theatre in Porthcurno. This spectacular open-air theatre was carved into a steep cliff overlooking the English Channel. The water below us was of a beautiful light blue colour. I found this interesting as there wasn't much sun that would help to make it that colour. The theatre itself was amazing too! As we made our way in we were surrounded by lots of different plants on both sides. I won't lie I did run at some points from the bees. Personally, I wish I had a bubble around me preventing the bees from getting close. Some parts of the theatre were really steep, making it hard to get up to the higher parts of it. As I'm not a big fan of heights I decided that the best thing for me to do would be to stay on the less steep levels. Good choice, I think.

After having Minack Theatre ticked off from our list we made our way to Land's End which was only a few minutes away. We went there in hopes of a better view of what was around. However, the fog was there again. This time it was not as bad, we could see more!

Whilst at Land's End I persuaded my parents to make our way to the very small Land's End Airport which connects with the Isles of Scilly only 20 minutes away by plane. I took some photos of the smallest passenger planes I ever saw. Even though it was only a 5 minute stop I was happy to be there. It was the opposite of the busy Manchester Airport.

Second on our list was Tintagel Castle, if you can even call it that. It felt more like a windy and scenic view of the Celtic Sea. To make our way across to the actual area where the castle was based, we had to cross a suspended bridge. Let me tell you I was not a big fan of it, considering the height it was suspended at. However, the most 'built up' part of the castle did show just how extraordinary it was to live in such an area hundreds of years ago. As we made our way around, I could not stop taking pictures of the waves that were crashing again the caves on the other side. It was something that I found really relaxing.

Third and last on our list of places to visit was St. Michael Mount. This was another castle which was on its own island which was connected to the mainland by a causeway which would be flooded at high tide, and you would have to take a boat across the causeway instead of walking on foot. Luckily, we didn't have to do that, but we did see some people get stuck right in the middle of it as the tide came in. I was laughing even though if I was in that situation I would not have been laughing.

The castle itself was giant but also beautiful. I'll never forget how hot it was walking around. Every bit of shade was a blessing.

Overall, I believe that this was time very well spent. It also means that we have most of the famous tourist attractions covered in Cornwall.

As we were leaving Cornwall to come back home, we stopped at Newquay Airport where I got to see a cool ramp for boarding onto a plane. It went up in a zigzag! There were also some planes in storage such as Thomas Cook A330 which most likely ended up there after the airline went into administration. We wanted to visit Newquay itself but due to a festival all connecting roads were blocked off.

Further up the country we also stopped at Cotswold/ Kemble Airport where many aircraft make their final journey before being made into cans or turned into cut-outs for us airplane fans. It was quite sad to see the number of planes that there was at the airport. Some of them were so old to the point where you would not find them flying around the world anymore.

23.
Plane spotting saga

If I wanted to be a good plane spotter, then I had to be at the airport more often doing what I love. Since, I lived an hour away I knew that this would not be easy. However, with some long persuading my parents agreed to take me to the airport once a month. Quite clearly that was the only offer that I could accept but it was a good one!

Since I was only going to the airport once a month, I knew I had to make the most of it and I believe I did. Just 2 hours at the airport would get me up to 500 photos that I could choose from. Although what was disappointing at first was that only about 100 photos would be any good for use, and that was under normal conditions. I'll never forget the day when I went to the airport and my camera lens was covered with dust spots that unfortunately appeared on the photos later when I came to edit them. I was so disappointed. As I later found out to remove the dust spots, I had to not clean the lens but the mirror inside the camera. It took me longer to figure out how to get access to it than the actual cleaning process took. Nevertheless, I was once again able to take beautiful photos at the airport.

Month by month I was taking photos of what I love most. That one day a month would be like a day spent in paradise.

Throughout this whole plane spotting saga, I was meeting amazing people that shared the same passion with me. What started with one person soon turned into a whole group of us. It was something quite unbelievable but also amazing!

24.
#friendsnotfollowers

During the early stages of the COVID pandemic I became really interested with the airline Ryanair. Something about it just stood out to me and I thought that I should create a 'fan page' for it. This enabled me to meet amazing people which shared the same passion in aviation as me. After some time, it led me to meet two amazing people Lays and Raees.

Raees also ran his own fan page but for the airline Emirates instead. As time went on we started speaking with each other more and more to the point where we were really good friends.

He introduced me to another amazing person Lays who is a devoted Emirates traveller. It was something fabulous to see her travel around the world with just one airline and sometimes not even leaving the airport but flying straight back to Dubai. Lays always referred to her audience as Friends Not Followers and it soon became a day that was celebrated every year.

One day Lays decided that to celebrate Friends Not Followers Day 2022 she would spend the weekend in Manchester. At this point me and Raees have been friends for two years, so we knew each other quite well. I've only ever spoke with Lays through messages, but I thought that this would be a perfect opportunity to spend a fabulous day together as a trio and get to know each other better. I wasn't wrong at all.

As we shared the same passion, we decided that we would visit the Concorde at Manchester Airport for a tour around it. Let me tell you that we hit the nail on the head. Our tour guide was a former Concorde pilot, so we were getting toured around by an expert. I was amazed! Towards the end of the tour inside the Concorde we were all invited to visit the flight deck. There must have been thousands of buttons all with different features. I could not image having to remember what each button was for.

During the tour of the plane, I was told that Raees and Lays booked tickets for a tour around Manchester City's Stadium. They invited me to come along too. During the tour of Concorde, I asked my parents to buy tour tickets for me too, so that I could join them. My parents agreed but under one condition, I would have to take my younger brother with me. What was highly unusual for me I agreed without a problem.

After the tour of Concorde our trio was picked up by Raees' older sister and we all went to Manchester City Stadium. As Lays referred to herself as a 'freak' she soon came up with her #freakchallenge which gained popularity on her social media. The #freakchallenge would always happen whenever Lays travelled somewhere across the world, it is the equivalent to a dare. As she came to Manchester, she was dared to shoot a penalty at Manchester United's pitch due to it having the same colour red as Emirates. Unfortunately, Manchester United's stadium was closed on that day, so Manchester City was the only option remaining.

Half an hour later we arrived in front of Manchester City. We made our way to the tour area where the big question had to be asked.

Would they allow Lays to shoot a penalty?

As we expected the answer was a 'No'. However, Lays could not disappoint her friends so eventually she was allowed to shoot on target in the 360° cinema. To me this showed that even if you get 'No' as an answer you should never give up.

25.
Scotland

In March of 2022 my dad found out that the was a friendly match happening between Scotland and Poland in Glasgow. It was the first time that a match like this was happening so close to us, and the tickets were at good prices so. We decided that we would all go and spend two days in Scotland.

In the early morning on March 24th we set off on our 5 hour journey to Glasgow in Scotland. I felt like the journey was going on for hours and hours. However, it was all worth it for the amazing scenery on the way. Mountains on both sides. It was like going through a valley but instead of a small country road it was a motorway going straight through the middle.

A few long hours later we were finally in Glasgow. We had a few hours before the match so we decided that we would have a small walk around Glasgow. I must say it was a truly beautiful city. The time that we spent walking around went by so fast that it was soon time to go back to the hotel to get changed and head for the football match.

Throughout my life I was never a huge football fan. Only during the big events would the football fan within me come alive. However, for this match I was really excited, I would finally see the Polish squad in real life. To make sure we got to the stadium on time we left about an hour early and it was a very good idea as the closer we got the busier the roads were.

A short drive later we arrived in the area where the stadium was. Our mission was to find a car park now and we did find an Asda car park, which would later turn out to be a big mistake.

Happily, we made our way towards the stadium. There must have been thousands of people that we walked past. Busy events such as this are not my type of thing. However, it was worth the sacrifice.

The match itself was filled with lots of excitement and finished with a draw.

At the end of the match part one of our big mistake with the car park became obvious. Lots of different people also parked there. It took us at least an hour to leave the car park, the same time it would have taken us to walk instead. Eventually we made our way out of it and were heading back to the hotel.

The next morning we woke up, got some breakfast and began to make our way to Edinburgh. Not without stopping at Glasgow Airport. The traffic might not have been the best and the photos but at least I could say that I have been there before.

The journey to Edinburgh was relatively short and soon we arrived at the base of Edinburgh Castle. We made it just in time for the One O'clock Gun which made me jump as I wasn't exactly sure when it would be fired.

The castle was massive. It took us around 3 hours to get through it. The part I found most interesting was the vault with the Scottish Crown Jewels. The vault itself was made from very thick metal and stone. Inside were the crown jewels including a crown, sceptre and sword.

Later we ate some extraordinary, delicious pizza which was shaped in a rectangle instead of a circle. It was ready in less than 5 minutes but was the best one I ever had.

On our way home it would not be a complete trip without stopping at Edinburgh Airport for some plane spotting. Even though I was taking pictures through a fence I managed to get some amazing photos. The lighting could not have been better too!

A few weeks after we came back home from our weekend trip part two of our big car park mistake became clear. We were fined for staying too long, most of which was caused by the delay we had in leaving the car park.

26.
Exploring the south

In April 2022, we thought it would be a good idea to finally complete our list of places to visit in the south of England and tie it in with the Easter break. On our list we had Durdle Door, Southampton and Arundel Castle.

On Friday afternoon we set off on our way to the south of England. Three hours later we arrived at our hotel for the night before heading to our places to visit.

The next morning, we left the hotel and began to make our way towards Durdle Door. On our way we decided to stop off at the Isle of Portland. The road connecting it had beautiful scenery, with the sea on both sides. Whilst exploring the isle I even got to see a military ship which I was very happy with.

Another hour later we arrived at Durdle Door. It did not feel like I was in England at all but rather somewhere in an exotic country. The view was beautiful on the path towards Durdle Door. It also gave me an adrenaline rush as the steep cliffs had no sort of fence to keep you from falling off. The adrenaline was worth it as I soon found out.

Once we took in all of the views and enjoyed the sun on the beach it was time to head to Southampton. I knew that Southampton had a busy port, so we decided to head to the port to see what it had to offer. My mum also wanted to see the 'port' but later it turned out that she was in fact thinking about the marine and not the big port. Let's say that when we arrived, we were all disappointed. There was nothing happening at all just water moving with the current. We decided not to wait and just watch the water move but instead go and explore a bit.

Without any aims we were exploring a historical part of Southampton when suddenly I realised that the car park would soon be closing. In a state of panic all of us rushed back to the car park. I was told that I would only be forgiven for this if one of the ships that was docked would be departing.

Luckily for me a cruise ship was setting off on its journey. I felt amazed at how big it was and just how close I was to it. At some points I could not even look at it as it would start to mess with my eyes due to the repeating pattern it had. To make this even more amazing the cruise ships in the port had a 'horn battle' between each other. It felt like a unique thing to experience. I definitely applied to the popular saying that goes along the lines of "Be grateful for the small things". As the ship was sailing off into the distance we left for our hotel in Arundel. We arrived there at late evening and went straight to sleep.

On Easter Sunday, we were woken up by the beautiful sunshine outside the window. As per usual we got our breakfast, packed our bags and left the stunning hotel room. The plan for today was to explore Arundel Castle and then I had a little plane spotting activity for myself on the way back home.

Arundel Castle itself was stunning and also very big. What I found surprising was that all of it was privately owned. At some points I felt like the tour of it would never end. However, I must say that all of it was worth the aching legs afterwards.

As a little plane spotting activity, we stopped at London Heathrow Airport. There was a plane flying over my head every 60 seconds. This is what I called paradise on Earth. Just 30 minutes got me 500 photos! I was so happy that I was at Heathrow that if possible I would just never leave. Unfortunately, that wasn't possible. Whenever a departing plane flew over my head I just thought to myself 'That's going to be me one day'.

The weekend break really didn't feel that short, but it was a good one! Next time we would be holidaying would be in Poland.

27.
Back in Poland

In early August of 2022, the 4th August specifically, it was finally time to set off for Poland. We have not been there for over a year and I could not have been more excited. As I was so excited about everything, I thought that I would document all of the amazing things that happened along the way with my friends on Instagram just like Lays does.

In the early hours of Friday, we departed for our long road trip to Poland. We drove to the Eurotunnel Terminal to cross under the English Channel. The train saved us over one hour compared to the ferry meaning we would get to our hotel in Germany faster. I was so happy that I would be able to sleep overnight rather than keeping on going to Poland.

Driving through France and a small part of Belgium went very smoothly until we got to Antwerp where the crazy traffic began. I'm not going to lie but at some points I thought that we would just never leave the city. The extreme temperature outside did not help a single bit. I guess this is what you get in very big cities at evening rush hour.

One hour later we were finally driving smoothly but not for too long. Just 30 minutes later we got into some traffic again. This time it was not due to the rush hour but a car somehow managed to drive onto a concrete roadside barrier. I could not help but laugh at how somebody managed to do that.

Another two hours later we arrived in Dortmund where we would stay for the night before carrying on with our journey tomorrow. Throughout this whole journey to Dortmund, I was putting everything that we did on my Instagram stories, and it would soon turn into something that I loved doing a lot. I even gave the German McDonald's a food review and I'm not lying when I say that it was much better than the UK. Afterwards we got back to the hotel as we had another long day ahead of us.

We woke up just before 9 in the morning, had breakfast and were ready to continue our journey through Germany and into Poland. We left the hotel just after 10am. From the moment we left, the weather was just getting worse with the rain intensifying. I already knew what this 9 hour drive would feel like forever, but the rain would make it feel even longer.

Driving through Germany always feels like a punishment for me. The drive makes me feel very restless. Afterall I am sat in a car doing nothing for hours and it feels like Germany will never end, the time for celebration starts when we arrive at the border.

Although this time our arrival at the border wasn't going to go smoothly. How can anything go so smoothly for so long? The motorway connection with Poland had lots of heavy traffic on it so we took a diversion. It soon turned out that the diversion led us to a closed road. Slowly but surely, we were running out of fuel and the nearest petrol station was across the border in Poland. I began to panic as we could not find any other route across the border.

Ten minutes later we found a different route and it looked very promising, straight into the city. It turned out to be good and just 15 minutes later we were finally in Poland. Even though this was a completely random feeling it was good to be stood on Polish soil and breathing in the Polish air.

As always, we ate some McDonald's at the border, exchanged money, fuelled up and continued with the last sector of our journey towards Bydgoszcz.

Two hours later we arrived at my grandparent's house and could finally celebrate my parent's wedding anniversary! The day was long and tiring so shortly we all went to sleep...

I was woken up by the already warm summer weather outside. The 6th August was my name day, these days are celebrated almost like your birthday in Poland and as always I felt like this was a very special moment. Especially this year as I was celebrating it in Poland.

The plan for the day was to meet up with a friend for breakfast that I haven't seen since 2019. We both agreed to have breakfast at one of the more popular restaurants in Bydgoszcz.

The breakfast was amazing, and it was great to see my friend again. To spend even more time together we decided to head towards the Bydgoszcz Old Town and Mill Island for a walk. Even though there is a 5 year age difference between us I did not even feel like there was a big age gap.

For the rest of the day, we celebrated my name day by going to the same restaurant with my family but for dinner instead. Once again it was delicious.

The 7th of August was the day that we would be leaving for our week stay at the seaside. We went to a popular but small seaside town. As our main aim was to spend the time at the beach we did not do too much exploring.

The best part of the day was always the evening when we would go to get a curled fry and then watch the sunset at the beach. Even though the closest airport was about an hour away I still got a little taste of my hobby but in a way I have never seen before. During one of the sunsets there was a plane flying over dragging an advertisement behind it.

I loved absolutely every minute of our stay at the seaside but now it was time to go and become a pilot, even if it was for a short while.

28.
Call me a pilot!

As a gift my auntie decided to hire a flight simulator for me where my flying skills would be put to the test. I was really excited for this from the moment I found out about it. The flight simulator was based on an Airbus A320, and the cockpit was fully to scale.

As I had 30 minutes of flying I had to make the most of it. I decided that as we were in Gdańsk I would do a circle around the airport there and then go to Madeira which is one of the world's most extreme airports to land at.

Whilst flying I felt like that was the perfect thing for me to do in the future. Although, all the other jobs in the aviation industry were still standing out to me. I really enjoyed every second of the flight simulator and was already looking forward to being there again whenever I could. It made me really feel as a pilot in control of a big plane with hundreds of passengers on.

Even though the simulator was fixed to the ground it did feel as if I was soaring through the air.

Very soon after that we went back to Bydgoszcz where we would soon find out that our car has broken, meaning we could not go back to England as we planned. I did not mind at all as it meant more time spent on holiday in Poland.

29.
This will be me in the future

Six months have flown by since I was last in Poland. However, it still felt like it was only yesterday.

In those six months not a lot of interesting things happened in my life. We just went on with our day to day lives with the occasional visit to a different city to see something.

However, as it was February it was time to fly for the week to Poland. I was extremely excited for this trip and annoyingly as the trip got closer the days felt longer. Although after a bit of a wait came the 21st of February and we were travelling to Poland.

On the 21st of February we woke up bright and early at 5am even though our flight departed at 10:20am. It's better to be early than late, especially for a flight that will not wait for you. I was very excited from the second that I woke up. It was my first flight in 3 years, and I would do anything to make it unforgettable.

Just before 7am we departed from Stoke and headed towards Manchester Airport. Our plan was to drive to the airport through all the little towns and villages instead of the motorway, we did not know how bad the morning traffic could be.

Unfortunately, Google Maps led us the wrong way and all the sudden we were driving on the A500, exactly where we did not want to end up. It was all going smoothly until we got past an intersection where the traffic came to a standstill. At first, I ignored it and hoped that we would get moving again. However, as time went on and we were still not moving I began to panic. Suddenly all the worst thoughts came rushing into my head.

We won't make the flight; it'll leave without us.

This is what our holiday will look like, stuck in traffic on the A500.

After 20 minutes of not moving people started to get out of cars and began walking. This was the moment when I thought that us not making the flight would be guaranteed...

Luckily just as everyone started to leave their cars we were moving again. It was such a moment of relief to be driving without any problems again. We exited the A500 at the next intersection and as originally planned we were driving through all the towns and villages.

A short while later we arrived at Manchester Airport Terminal 3. I was feeling very excited and could not wait any longer to officially begin the trip.

Our suitcase was dropped off at check-in and we went towards security. This was the point where I felt quite saddened as we had to say goodbye to my dad who unfortunately could not come with us this time.

As we headed further into security, we kept waving at each other until we were no longer able to see each other.

Security went very smoothly, and we were soon through into the duty-free area. We found some seats but shortly after decided to head to the shops to pick out a gift for my grandparents.

One payment later we were ready to depart to Poland.

The flight was departing in an hour so we decided to head towards the gate area from where our flight would depart. It was so full when we got there that we headed in the opposite way to find somewhere to sit. I found the perfect seat for myself overlooking the departing and arriving planes, but the airport then went very quiet meaning I did not get to see a lot of planes.

About an hour later an announcement said that our flight was beginning to board. Although my trusted Flightradar24 app was saying that the plane was still 20 minutes away and it was nowhere to be seen on the ground. Though we decided to go with the flow and wait at the gate for the plane to arrive.

Then a 'Final Call' announcement came on, but the plane was still 10 minutes away. I was starting to get annoyed with the delay and everything was beginning to ache, I was stood still for almost 30 minutes with a backpack on my back and the duty-free shopping in my hands.

Finally, the plane made contact with the ground and made its way towards the gate. People on the arriving flight quickly got off and we were able to get on.

I felt great walking on the apron and up the stairs to the plane. My head suddenly cleared of everything else that was going on around me and focused on the adventure ahead.

As I boarded the plane I gave a letter for the pilot to one of the flight attendants and asked them if they could pass the letter on to the pilot. The flight attendant was amazing and said that she would pass it on.

I felt so happy to be flying that it's hard to explain what I was feeling at that moment.

Just 20 minutes later we were soaring high above the clouds.

About an hour before we landed the flight attendant that I gave the letter to handed me the letter back and said that the captain invites me to the cockpit after we land.

As soon as I noticed that the crew were finishing up with their service I got up from my seat and started to give out the thank you cards and lollies to each of them. They were so happy with them, and I was happy that I made their day even just a bit brighter. Afterwards, I got a picture with all crew which I will treasure forever.

During the whole flight I felt like this was the right thing for me. That was what I would want to do in the future. At the end I went to the cockpit where I got to talk with the first officer and got lots of photos.

I was the last passenger to get off the plane along with my mum and little brother. Just before passport control one of the duty-free bags slipped out of my hand and everything inside of it smashed. This meant that we were left without a gift but also meant that I was in some big trouble.

30.
He looks at home

After an amazing week in Poland during which we went to a few restaurants, went shopping, met up with my friend and celebrated my mum's birthday, it was time to head back home. This would be on a flight again this time from Bydgoszcz to Bristol. As always, I was really excited about this. Even if it meant leaving Poland. Although I would not mind staying for a day or two more.

My grandparent's house was only located 15 minutes away from the airport unlike an hour back in the UK. Considering that the airport was also quite small it meant arriving only about an hour before the flight departed.

We arrived at the airport went through check-in and then waited in a lengthy security line. There was only one lane open making the process very long. Soon, I began to get fed up with the wait. On my back I was carrying a heavy backpack filled with books that we bought, making the wait even more tiring and annoying. Once through security we bought some things at duty free and before we knew it the plane arrived. We boarded the plane and once again I gave a letter to the flight attendant so that they could pass it on to the pilot. I sat down in my seat and was ready for the flight. Excitement was buzzing within me.

The whole flight was amazing! I got a reply to my letter, and it was returned to me during the flight. Each flight attendant was once again given a lolly and a thank you note.

As I was walking up and down the cabin aisle, I just imagined what it would feel like if that was me in the future. I must say I felt quite good doing that.

To make the flight even more amazing I got to have a photo with the crew, and they even gave me a little gift. I felt so happy to be there with them!

Unfortunately, the flight had to come to an end and soon we landed in Bristol. I went to the cockpit where the pilot was waiting for me. What I noticed in both cockpits was that everything was very small, it almost looked like a toy. Interestingly, the cockpit onboard the Boeing 737-800 is one of the smallest in commercial planes.

The pilot was amazing and even lit up everything in the cockpit for the photos. When I was sitting in the pilot's seat, I felt like that would be me even more than it the role of a flight attendant. It was a fabulous feeling!

When later showing this photo to one of my teachers in school I was described as looking as if 'I was at home'. This was the one phrase that led me to believe that nothing will be able to stop me from becoming a pilot in the future. I just had to work for it.

As we landed in Bristol, we had a 3 hour drive back home to Stoke and I was once again reunited with my dad.

From the moment I left the airport I was already looking forward to my next flight!

31.
Today is just the beginning!

Looking ahead in your teenage years may be hard for some. Although for me this is not the case.

Ever since those two flights in February of 2023, I've been looking ahead and into the future even more than I have ever before. However, I cannot just credit those two flights.

My grandad was a pilot when he was young. He might not have been a commercial pilot like I hope to be one day, but I still look up to him. In some cases, I even hope to take similar steps as he did.

When I reach the end of my education here in the UK I hope to move back to Poland and to Bydgoszcz specifically. This is where I will study for my Private Pilot License (PPL) which will enable me to move onto my next step.

My next step that I will hope to take will be to go to the same university as my grandad did. Although, instead of taking the military route I hope to take the commercial route. This form of learning will save me more than £90,000 compared to the UK and will still leave me with the same qualifications at the end.

Now I must wait and see if I'll be able to reach my dream and gain my wings!

Welcome to the end of my book!

Dear Reader,

I would like to thank you lots for taking the time to read my book, *Jakub*. I hope you enjoyed reading it as much as I enjoyed writing it. If you liked the book, then I invite you to leave a review on Amazon and share it with your friends.

I would like to thank Tracey Leese, author of *Teach Like a Queen* who supported me along the way with this book. Thank you for helping with anything that I could not do.

Thank you to my parents who never stopped believing in me whilst writing this book. Your support will always be appreciated.

Thank you to everyone that wrote a book endorsement, you are greatly appreciated!

Thank you to anyone else that helped with this book! It would not be possible without your help.

If you wish to contact me, you can find me here:

Instagram: @jakub_thebook
Twitter: @jakub_thebook

Once again thank you!

Jakub

Printed in Great Britain
by Amazon

21189840R10052